THE
SMART MONKEY
HANDBOOK

75+ Quick Tips for Young People

A Quick Companion Guide for Young People

A PRACTICAL GUIDE FOR THE MIND AND BODY

MARK BODWALK

Contents

Acknowledgments	v
Dedication	1
The Quick Guide	3
Character Foundations	5
Relationships	17
Mind, Body, Health, Spirituality	25
Transitions	41
Good Advice	55
Closing and Final Thoughts	65
Dear Young Reader	67
Dear Older Reader	69
Notes	71
About the Author	145

© The Smart Monkey Handbook:
For Young People
Copyright 2024 by Mark Bodwalk
www.markbodwalk.com
Published by Mark Bodwalk
ISBN: 978-1-7352471-4-4

All rights reserved. No part of this publication may be reproduced, distributed, or transmitted in any form or by any means, including photocopying, recording, or other electronic or mechanical methods, without the prior written permission of the author. This publication is designed to provide accurate and authoritative information about the subject matter covered. The advice and strategies contained herein may not be suitable for your situation. You should consult with a professional when appropriate.
The advice and strategies found within this book may not be suitable for every situation. This work is sold with the understanding that neither the author nor the publisher are held responsible for the suggestions made, nor the results accrued from the advice herein. Before starting any regimen, always consult a licensed professional.

Formatting by Tracee Garner,
Garner Solutions, LLC
© Cover Design by Fiverr.com/sam_4321

Acknowledgments

Acknowledgements

To all of the many people I encountered and encountered me while I was in the vast uncertain experience of growing up whom graciously or reluctantly lent me a hand. This book is a quick summarized thank you note to them and results from their help and is my attempt to return the favor to all those who come after me. I appreciate the many people that took an interest in me and took action to direct me. What follows is a humble, minuscule and basic acknowledgement of some of what was taught to me.

Dedication

Heartfelt and incomprehensible gratitude I give to my good parents that had me and got me on the planet. Impossible odds, and the least I can do to honor them is to show that I learned something useful to pass on and didn't waste their time or squander the gift of life they gave to me.

The Quick Guide

It is 2024 and beyond by now, why hasn't there been a book like this one yet? What kind of book? A rule book, a basic helpful handbook, that is a simple heads-up check list to guide and orient a young person toward the responsibilities which are rapidly approaching.

Growing into adulthood is challenging enough, plus meeting all of the benchmarks: this reading is intended to make the challenges less difficult by recognizing and anticipating them, and having more preparedness.

You can never say, after reading this book, *"Why didn't anyone tell me about this…?"* because it's in this book! You will have no more excuses. In this book, you know, your book of foundational tools for living, there are lined note pages in the back for you to record your development, growth and process the meaning you give to your life experiences.

We rely almost solely on coaches, uncles, aunts, teachers, cousins, parents to reach down and pull up young people to or even beyond where we needed to be three years ago. The family dinner table may not be enough any longer to supply developing young minds with the values, morals, motivation, habits, logical thinking, ethics, decision-making skills and implant critical thinking abilities so crucial for young people to be able to think independently. Whoever is teaching you to avoid stepping on the land mines, falling off the cliffs of life and giving you specific suggestions to make your life better, more fulfilling and meaningful, want to be sure you are apprised of what will help in your life.

Here are a few concepts to help you so you can reassure those that are helping you. You probably know the concepts in this quick guide already, but like all advice, it bears repeating for the next generation who may like it quick and to the point on the journey into adult life.

Buckle up!

Character Foundations

Weak Points: Note your weak points or where you feel unsure or lack confidence. This is where you will need to go to grow. To grow at something you must have fun doing it no matter how challenging the learning. Passions can flip to weak points if they are pursued in an unbalanced way and become obsessive.

Goals: Remember to remember what your personal goals are. For example: good manners, humor, maturity, being well read, self-discipline, able to make small repairs, punctual, self-control, time management, thoughtful, good communication skills.

Vocabulary: Have a full range of vocabulary and know the right word to use. You don't have to be an English major but don't dumb down either. Know the right word to express your feelings. Using too many words will sound pretentious. As with nature, find the balance in all things. Use the vocabulary appropriate to the topic area you are discussing, i.e., politicians have constituents not folks. Pilots fly at altitudes not heights. Lawyers represent clients not people.

Authentic: Commit to being honest and authentic. The world has enough insincerity and con artists taking advantage of others. Have integrity, class and a good reputation. This is genetics, upbringing and a decision.

Procrastination: Putting off or intentional delay is a poor time management technique and not a recipe for success, pride or accomplishment. Now is Universal Time. Prioritization is an important factor but not avoidance or delay.

Self-Development: When you are older you won't want to feel that life was a rip-off, a big waste of time or that you were cheated. Develop yourself and skills now: discipline, patience, philosophy, spirituality, good habits, compassion, social skills and interests, so you will have lots to fall back on to keep you busy and bursting with pride in later life.

Self-Responsibility: Most of the problems we have are a result of our own actions and decisions. Develop confidence and the ability to access data quickly and work decisively in the moment and trust your intuition. Sometimes a single moment will be all the time we have for a quick decision that will have ramifications well into the future. Not all decisions come with the luxury of time. "Many things that happen to us are the result of a decision that we made when we were very young." —Dustin Hoffman

Bad Habits: Be aware of developing bad habits; they can silently accumulate and last a lifetime. Cast them away as they tempt you before they take hold. Trust your intuition. You know when something is good or bad for you. Bad habits usually appear when we have a weakness in some area. Have good habits: resist peer pressure, think for yourself and you don't need to be cool, act tough or turn people's heads. What you need is not on the internet. You need clear knowledge of who you are and to have integrity. Bad habits for example: procrastinating, poor speech, telling lies or half-truths, avoidance, manifesting anger, poor impulse or emotional control, bad manners and using people damages yourself and your public image. Once ingrained and routine, bad habits are more challenging to dispel. Like shorts cuts, bad habits are always harmful, in spite of their seductive allure, will never treat you well or be a friend in the end. Your character is your best friend. Here is a list of some more bad habits you want to avoid: not returning borrowed items, being crass, poor eye contact, not reading a room as you enter, not planning, neglecting your teeth, borrowing money, not helping, interrupting, eating too fast, being selfish, forgetting manners, dominating conversation, not asking how someone is, being loud, forgetting things, being disorganized, not thoughtful, turning in poor work, driving carelessly, not anticipating, procrastination, poor listening, not following through, being late, dismissing people's feelings, acting aloof, poor hygiene and irregular sleep habits just to name a few. As with this life, turn the bad habits around and into the good behaviors you want.

Painful Experiences: Remember both the good and the bad experiences and learn from them. Repeating bad experiences over and over and missing or forgetting the learning is much too painful a way to go through life. There is winning and learning. If there is losing, then the learning is lost.

Language Speaks: Language precedes you and reveals who you are. Being vague, sloppy or indefinite is not in your best interests. Avoid slang, and the overused words of the day. Adopting the common phraseology to fit in is dumbing down and is lazy, weak, sheep like and cheap. Swear words are an overused unimaginative way to pretend to fit in, be familiar, cool and hip, are not compelling and often masks illiteracy. Besides, only the French know how to elevate using obscenities to an art form. Plus it is difficult to turn off common vernacular, swearing and bad habits in a professional setting. Be original and enunciate clearly with precision. Use the right word and skip vulgar, lazy, over used obscenities as they are not positive, are degrading and have no useful purpose. Follow and use correct rules of grammar. Having an identity and fitting in would be poorly served without your own distinctive, uplifting, signature language style and uniqueness. Use some precision and the vocabulary of the subject you are talking about. Avoid cliches like the plague. "The difference between the almost right word and the right word is really a large matter—it's the difference between the lightning bug and the lightening." -Mark Twain

Reputation: Help people know you as the kind, nice, mannered even-tempered person you are.

Sloppiness: It is easy to exhibit poor language, posture and self-care and allow it to seep into other facets of our lives. Isomorphic.

Isomorphic: Corresponding or similar in form and relations.

Reliability: Do what you'll say and say what you will do. "Don't let down the people that depend on you."-- George Harrison

Limitations: Not everyone can dance or sing in key, but we all can rise above our limitations.

Housekeeping: Wash clothes in cold water using an unscented chemical free detergent. Avoid dry cleaning your clothes. You do not need to have residual chemicals rubbing on your skin all day and night. Give your liver a rest from clearing all the toxins that your body is exposed to every day, already. Wash your new clothes before you wear them for the same reason. New clothes are exposed to pesticides, sizing, stiffeners and fragrances. Keep a clean and organized home. Take your shoes off and wash your hands when you come in. Neatness and organization is gratitude.

Bravery: Accept and respect the inevitable pain, loss, sadness and despair in the human experience. "I don't know why people fear death, life can be so much more painful." —Helen Keller

Good Decision-Making: Be able to size up, evaluate and make sound, sometimes life-long planet-orbit changing decisions of immense magnitude, as well as small quick choices. Learn to trust your intuition, information and data-analyzing skills and your good robust common sense. Sometimes decision-making is easy without even having to consider the options: just follow the right, best and safest path. Be conscious of other people's feelings or trying to be a hero. When there is doubt in a course of action, there is no doubt, just do the right, safest thing. The results of a decision can be regrettable for two reasons: we did something we shouldn't have, or we did not do something we should have. Weigh out all possible consequences before deciding. Having regret for something we did or did not do as a result of our decision can play out for a lifetime and be very painful.

Language: Avoid too much slang, obscenities and poor sentence construction that is choppy and difficult to follow. Be coherent and fluent. Follow the rules of grammar, tell a good story and captivate listeners with descriptive imagery. Good inspiring books to read: Treasure Island, Alice in Wonderland, Through the Looking Glass, Red Harvest, and The lion, the Witch and the Wardrobe and of course any classic works including books by Earnest Hemingway, the most precise and economical of all writers.

Neatness: Keep your things neat and organized so you can find something. This shows gratitude and discipline and will serve you well as your life enlarges in scope. So develop the habit early. It is so unnecessary and sad having to wait while someone who is late and searching through a mess to find something. Remember Isomorphic, if something is happening on the micro level, it often happens on the macro-life level.

Cool: No matter which way the pendulum of the decades swing, the word cool will always be synonymous with, style, grace, confidence, class, reserve, restraint, nice, proper, manners and integrity.

Discouragement: If you feel driven and are pursuing something that you know is right, don't be discouraged or give up because of adverse factors or difficult people. This is a character factor about perseverance and believing in yourself. No one ever succeed by quitting and giving up on themselves. "Winners never quit, and quitters never win." —Vince Lombardi. "Believe you can, and you are halfway there."—Theodore Roosevelt. "Believe you can or believe you can't you are right either way." —Henry Ford.

Reputation: You should not have to give a thought about your reputation especially if you behave well and don't take advantage of people.

Dismissiveness: No need to have the off-handed habit of being dismissive. There is value and something to learn and grow from everything and everyone. The same goes for condescension: talking down to someone doesn't make others look up to you.

Greedy: If you have something and you don't think it is enough, don't risk what you already have to try and get some more. Be grateful for what you have.

Nice: It is nice to be important but more important to be nice.

Inferiority, Superiority: Feeling superior or inferior are the same. Both derive from fear, fear of not being good enough. You are good enough, but you must think and act as such.

3 Characteristics: There are many characteristics of an adult but three primary ones: ability to self-soothe. You are not a baby, have a little bit of a thick skin and buckle up. Next, have emotional control. Finally, be able to put yourself in the other person's shoes, have compassion, empathy and understand their point of view.

Self-Discipline: Is such an important key and it will fit all of your locks.

The Smart Monkey Handbook:

The following is a checklist of concepts that can help structure a young person's development into adulthood and beyond:

- Impulse control
- Honesty
- Respectfulness
- Self-reflection
- Emotional control
- Personal hygiene
- Reading comprehension
- Positive
- Empathy
- Self-care
- Decision making
- Coherence
- Orderliness
- Focus
- Self-discipline
- Time management
- Ordered thought
- Command of language
- Considerate
- Sensitivity
- Know your boundaries
- Kindness
- Accurate reporting
- Politeness
- Give compliments
- Don't attack
- Gratitude

- Generosity
- Humility
- Patience
- Compassion
- Listen
- Manners
- Inner peace
- Punctuality
- Manage social media
- Good Judgment
- Resist peer pressure
- Think for yourself
- Master inter and intra personal conflict
- Good speaking, concise phrasing
- Respect for self, elders, parents, authority figures
- Withhold projections
- Positive-presence
- Planning

Hypocrisy: People acting one way and saying something else and awash in contradictions are sadly common place. Note the occurrence, they are struggling and have lost their footing. Be understanding and avoid the credibility-diminishing practice in your behavior.

Victim or Martyr: Avoid both, neither is an identity nor compelling.

Charisma: Exude self-confidence, warmth and caring. Be attentive, notice details and show interest. Chitchat. Hold a room without being the center of attention. Be approachable. Approach others. Talk to different people, make connections and eye contact, everyone is important. No snobbiness. Enjoy yourself, laugh, be present, positive and have a presence. Don't appear preoccupied or irritable as if you don't want to be there. Want to be where you are and make yourself at home and be comfortable. Resist being pretentious and having airs and be fun and laugh at yourself a little. Be charming, candid and spontaneous. Ask deeper, not prying questions that invite meaningful, revealing, thoughtful responses that foster connection. Don't be quick to make the conversation about yourself to showcase your accomplishments. A lot of having charisma is about showing restraint, respect and interest in others. Show that you are listening and care. Connect. Convey sincerity, graciousness and humility. No need to be bubbly with one-liners, just open yourself up to someone, give them the benefit of the doubt and indicate that they are important.

Daily Distractions - The daily distractions of everyday life can be fun and amusing or overwhelming and distracting. In either case, always keep in mind your long-term goals and aspirations. "Where focus goes, energy flows." - Tony Robbins

Cherish – Cherish the small things. Treasure the simple pleasures.

Relationships

Finding a Mate: Find a mate that will help you to reach your goals in life and will remain with you. Don't wait too long so that you can grow together from the star, and not waste too much time revolving your life around, clubs, dancing, sex, romance and going out indefinitely. Going into your 30's after having had some fun and travel is a good time to be settled. King Charles was not a good role model in this area. Better settle in with potential life partner sooner rather than later so you can grow together.

Friends: Everything you enjoy and accomplish will mostly be with and because of friendships and people. The people around you will teach you the most about yourself. Help them, comfort them and be a good friend to them. A relationship is a two-way exchange. Know the other person's time line, where they came from, what they did, when, what order and what happened along the way.

Friends Again: Go out of your way to keep the friends you make when you are young. These will be the people who will know you best along with family members and will be one of your greatest assets. One can't make lifelong friends when you are older and new friends are not always easy to make, so make lifelong friends while you are young and out meeting people. Good friends should last a lifetime. Know as many different types of people as possible and don't be a snob. Learn about, help, know, eat with and understand people from different cultures. Be non-judgmental and you will learn the most about life and yourself from other people. Let them teach you. They will need to be accountable but that is their job not yours. Just make sure you are accountable to them. Holding friends too accountable without a little humor and lightness is being a schoolmarm.

Genders: Make a point to understand the other gender and other orientations. Just by listening, paying attention, avoiding stereotypes and judgment will help you understand yourself also.

Being Used: If you realize you are being used or taken advantage of: first determine if there is some benefit in it for you. No need to be outraged.

Friends Need Leeway: Avoid holding your friends too accountable. Show forgiveness, leniency and some latitude. No one needs to be perfect. Show some understanding and have compassion for the difficulty of the human condition through your friends. You would like them to return the same understanding, forgiveness and latitude when you make a mistake or are late. You are just as young and inexperienced about being responsible and accountable as they are. Show them how big you are and have a laugh. They don't need another big brother, father or mother in you. Show compassion and patience. They, like you, have had enough threats, middle school assistant principals and coaches.

Good Listener: Be thoughtful listener. Listen to their heart and what they have to say. The heart never lies. It speaks the truth, good, bad or indifferent. Listen from your own heart.

Boundaries: Be mindful of the limits of your physical, emotional and psychological space with others. Mind your own business, respect all people, their things and feelings and don't cross over lines without permission no matter how familiar you think you are. Ask first before helping someone. Be mindful of your transactions with other people and their space. Boundaries are the basic understanding of how we relate to others. Boundary crossings become boundary violations easily. Good fences make good neighbors.

Relationships: You will be in a good relationship when it is positive, fun, feels good and you are growing, learning, up lifting the other and vice versa, while admiring the other person as they admire you.

Grievances with Others - Patch up your relationship misunderstandings quickly and make them right. It helps no one and proves no point to punish someone with silence and ill feelings. Adult life is difficult enough. Reach out, mend fences.

Intimacy: Intimacy, trust, respect, safety, non-judgment and romance are all connected. Be careful about your sexual circuity running your brain.

Leaders: Don't trust the leaders, watch the parking meters." —Bob Dylan

Jealous Friends: If your friends are jealous of you, then you are probably on the right track, and they are probably not your friends.

Peer Group: Your peer group may have some personnel changes now and then but keep them a priority and keep it positive. Going through the stages and experiences of life with other close friends is beyond rewarding.

Peer Pressure/Group Thinking: If everyone is doing, thinking, eating something, consider that it may be wrong. Think against the grain, think outside the box and think for yourself reflecting your values. Develop your judgment criteria, thinking and intuition and learn to trust yourself. Group thinking is not always right. Group dynamics can overcome individual values to great detriment.

Trusted Friend: It is fortunate to have a good trusted non-judgmental person to talk to. This ability to connect to someone and them to you is crucial and makes life so much better and the absence of which can be devastating.

Making New Friends: When you meet and want to know a person and make a new friend, go slowly, breathe, take your time and be relaxed. Don't overstate yourself and act hyper. Remain being yourself and spontaneous, don't try too hard or take on some other persona and self-consciousness will melt away just as with any other situation. Breathe and put yourself at ease. We can meet people socially or virtually. Social media or meeting actual living, breathing, warm blooded people like yourself. Tend toward genuine, relationships to keep your social skills current and sharp with real human beings. Be a real people person not a social media half-hidden, artificial mystery person ghosting and spouting catch phrases disappearing and reappearing. Social media experiences are not real.

Comfort Friends: Of course, comfort your friends, especially when they are in need, distressed, feeling down or sick. Don't let them down when they need you the most, and in fact, never let them down especially when it is inconvenient for you. We need to make these sacrifices as we would like to have them made for us.

Jealously, Bullying: If others are making fun of you, they are probably jealous and have a lot of other problems to distract themselves from and acting out and bullying you is nothing personal although it certainly seems personal. Some family dysfunction at home is likely at the core of their problem, not you. If they weren't bullying you, they would find someone else close by. You were just convenient for them. Above all don't be rattled by them and get upset which is what they want to show their power and see if you were willing to give your power to them. Laugh it all off if anything. Make them your friends of sorts, they're lonely. They are likely cowards with pent up feelings of inferiority from a dysfunctional home life.

Being Dismissed: Same as above: don't take feeling dismissed or a lack of consideration or attention personally. People are busy, distracted, preoccupied and tired with plenty of their own problems. Remain poised, respectful and present. Don't buy into their indications that you are not important because they want you to go away.

Acknowledge: Thank, recognize and appreciate the efforts of others that contribute to your life. No one makes it on their own without help from others.

B.O.D: Give others the benefit of the doubt. Don't be stingy with your good will and bigness. Assume others will do well and meet your expectations even if they don't. Your expectations influence the outcome of others. They are human just like us all: stumbling down the path to enlightenment.

To get to know someone new:

- See them under stress
- Study them is they are intoxicated, their best and worst traits will be exaggerated
- Get to know their parents and observe their interaction
- Observe them with their mother
- Give them a little bit of power and observe what they do with it
- Observe their relationship with time
- Observe their relationship with money
- Note how they behave when disappointed
- See them upset and angry
- See how they regard private information
- Play a competitive sport with them
- Eat a sit down meal with them
- Observe leadership, boundaries, spontaneity and teamwork and how they treat the wait staff.

Personal Disputes: Most interpersonal disputes resolve just by each person feeling understood.

Break Ups: Are inevitable and not a referendum on your self-worth or value but could be a report card on character and behavior. The least caring and invested person in the relationship will control it. Just be sure the breakup was not because of your behavior: lazy, sloppy, insincerity, inattentiveness, not caring or were selfish, inconsiderate or exhibited poor or immature behavior, character or thoughtlessness. Admiration for the other person is the key element required for a successful relationship. Never have a bad breakup, always exhibit class, dignity, respect and restraint. Be grateful for what you leaned and honor the experiences you shared and time spent together.

Friendships: "It's fine and necessary to move beyond your friends but not away from them." —Abraham Lincoln

Mind, Body, Health, Spirituality

Critical Thinking: Think outside the box and non-traditionally but use caution when expressing your views publicly since thinking unconventionally and not drinking the Kool Aid may label you as difficult, a threat or a behavior problem. Learn to think for yourself and in your own way to develop a rational which will help prevent you from being easily persuaded and taken advantage of.

Loneliness: There will be times in your life when a feeling of being alone and misunderstood engulfs you. This will pass and you will have learned about yourself, understand compassion, humility and gratitude. Embrace the lonely moments and despair without distraction or avoidance or drugs which would only raise loneliness to alienation and beyond manageable. Alcohol, so common to use to self-medicate, teaches disconnection and will waste the opportunity for growth and self-reflection. Avoid legal fees, be kind to your liver and don't follow conventional thinking that aloneness is a bad condition. You may move closer to self-understanding. This is where poets find their imagery, philosophers their meaning and scientists their insights.

Nature: Remain close to nature, where all of the designs, structures, laws, beauty and life reside. The further we move away from nature, the unhealthier we become. This is true of food, thinking, behavior, medicine, habits, living, everything. Nature is simple in its elegance, structured in its designs, breathtaking in its beauty, provides us with all things and is the ultimate teacher. "Study nature, love nature, stay close to nature. It will never fail you."—Frank Lloyd Wright

Health: Make your health and teeth a practice and a priority early on. Many health problems are self-induced over time by neglect, lack of priorities, being too busy or bad habits. There are no short cuts in life, and this is your life. Perform the maintenance and work required. Again no short cuts which are always more expensive and take more time in the long run. Your body is rented from nature and the better you take care of it before you have to turn it in, the more you will enjoy your life's experience.

Self-Care: Self-care is not selfish. Non-self-care is selfish requiring others to take care of you. Self-care is always an exercise in balance. No need to be a fanatic, neurotic or hypochondriac. Use good common basic sense to take care of yourself. Give from your surplus not your reserves to avoid depletion. Offer compassion and patience from your heart, not anger and resentment to avoid burn out.

Posture: Maintaining good posture is a statement about your self-worth to yourself, and to others. Posture conveys: openness, availability, receptivity, mood, health, energy, confidence, self-awareness, comfort, attitude and self-worth. Sloughing does not look or feel good in any way and crowds your internal organs and is counter to the benefits of yoga. Always sit up straight and maintain the lumbar curve in your lower back.

Birth Control: Take charge of birth control, it is not the other person's responsibility. Nothing interferes more with life's trajectory than children at the wrong time or too soon no matter how cute you think they are. Career before kids. To do otherwise often results in generational poverty, and child support checks which are bad for everyone, especially the child. More education, fewer children. Marrying someone to have children with and divorcing them later is beyond comprehension. It is selfish and an ultimate cruelty for everyone involved. Children make a good marriage better and a bad marriage worse. The best birth control is confidence, self respect, self esteem and a career path.

Hormones: A responsible, developed, disciplined and mature person maintains control of their emotions, desires, drives, passions and behaviors. Learn this early and remain in control of yourself. The sense of pride, dignity, mastery and integrity that develops from self-control is our ultimate core accomplishment.

Humor: It is fun and helpful to have a sense of humor, some cynicism and be irreverent occasionally. Life can be so strange, shocking, surprising without comic relief or irony.

Wisdom: "Be not the first by whom the new are tried nor yet the last to lay the old aside." —Alexander Pope

Conscientiousness: Be kind, compassionate, considerate, conscientious, do good work and more than is expected. The opposite action controls the world, wreaks havoc and degrades the living experience for everyone.

Plays, Symphonies, Opera: To rescue yourself from drowning in the mind numbing sea of trending pop culture distractions, and stave off mediocrity, keep yourself grounded in the Classics. Attend cultural events to keep you engaged in your community.

Lachrymose: If you feel sad, lost or don't care, make a decision not to be. It is that simple. Same goes for depression. It is that simple also. If you feel lethargic, move. Expressing energy creates energy, again,

"Nothing happens without movement." —Albert Einstein

Continuity: Notice the continuity and flow of all things. One thing, person, event or idea leads into another and another and another, endlessly.

Fast Foods: Steer away from the slow death of fast, industrial, processed, indefinite shelf-life, artificial and adulterated fake food, which is intended to make profits and addictions, not healthy people. Fast food can shorten your life span and cause you to be sick at sixty. Remember going into the entrance of any hospital starts when you are very young by walking in the door of any fast food so-called restaurant. Start your healthy eating discipline early in life before bad lazy habits become habituated and fast food addiction takes hold. Developing this regimen and self respect will serve you well in other areas of your life. Again, isomorphic.

Dental Hygiene/ Financial Concerns: Exercise excellent dental hygiene. Teeth should last a lifetime, so take care of your teeth and gums now daily while you are young, you will be so glad you did when you are old. This is an expression of the same self-care and discipline that you apply in other areas. Gargle with warm salt water, not with commercial mouthwash as it destroys beneficial oral pre-digestive enzymes. The degree of care you provide for your teeth will be equivalent to how well you care for your finances. It will be isomorphic—corresponding or similar in form and relations.

Care for Yourself: Please don't rely on the government to take care of you. Government is a complicated bureaucratic entity with very little phone support that works slowly and will show little caring or compassion. Take care of your own needs first and then use government services as a final desperate option.

Care for Your Finances: Like good health practices, be attentive to your finances, earnings, savings and invest even a small portion of your earnings. This will safeguard your financial future and make you fiscally responsible. There's nothing wrong with indulging but have restraint. "Neither a borrower nor a lender be, for loan oft loses both itself and friend...." —Polonius "Beware of little expenses; a small leak will sink a great ship." —Benjamin Franklin

Disappointment: Remember to remain grateful, humble and big. Everything will go your way most of the time and above all, you are still on a nice, green spinning planet with a clear blue sky and you are alive. Keep your perspective. When one door closes, fourteen more will open. Disappointment and rejection present other opportunities and are an integral part of life. Handle all disappointment with style, grace and class. "Expectations are the waiting room for disappoint."--RFK, Jr. Everything that happens is potentially the best thing that could ever but you have to make it so.

Wisdom: Watch, study and observe older people. They may seem out of touch in so many ways with many contradictions, but they can teach invaluable lesson and tell stories that give you perspective. An end-of-life person will reveal what is important to know: humility, compassion and gratitude. When you are older you won't need to read this book, that's why you are reading it now so that getting older will be a little smoother.

About Abraham Lincoln: "The man is the sum total of his contradictions."—William Seward, the President's Secretary of State

Overcome Your Resistance: When you find yourself doing something that you need to do but don't really want to do, you are on the right track of self-discipline. While practicing piano, cleaning, studying; ask yourself, "What else would I be doing that is better for my future." Besides, anything put off only has to be completed later when you have less time or inclination and even more to do. Stay ahead of your needs and then after the pride of accomplishment, pursue your wants. You can play later; life is best played as a long game. Good sound advice.

Danger vs. Recklessness: We all know the thrill of fear turning into excitement, as on a rollercoaster when you feel so alive. Danger turning into recklessness and tragedy in a second is not exciting or thrilling in any way.

Now: Life is a not dress rehearsal for later like practicing for a school play. Life is in the present moment, now. Make it count!

Momentum: Have a healthy respect for the unsentimental, profound and sometimes cruel forces of nature and gravity and the power behind movement. Nature presents a dazzling and breathtaking spectacle of beauty and wonderment and the power to drive the cosmos with an unseen force and take your breath away which we often take for granted. Nature or life does not entertain the concept of fairness or watching out for you and favors no one but gave you all the tools and potential you will need to reach old age meaningfully.

Observe and Write: When you feel awed by beauty or moved by sentiment, write a poem about how you feel and stay connected to yourself.

Journal: It's good to keep a journal, many people do. You may want to refer to it to remember your feelings and emotions, both pleasant and during bouts of adversity. A journal will hold you accountable, teach you to write, stimulate your memory, help you articulate your thoughts and feelings. It will become a record of your growth, your life and keep you thinking. "Reading makes a full man, speaking makes ready man, writing makes a thinking man." —Francis Bacon.

"Either write something worth reading or do something worth writing."—Ben Franklin

Edible Food-Like Substances: All of the edible food-like poisons, chemicals and additives in your processed food products and medicines you eat and skin care products you apply has enrolled you in a large food science experiment as a cohort without your permission or informed consent. Again this is not Germany where it is illegal and inconceivable to conduct food science experimentation on humans. Cancer researchers are telling us that cancer may be genetic. This may be true, but the likelihood of cancer coming from lifestyle, industrial chemicals and environmental poisons is more likely.

Breathing: When in a painful or strained situation, draw a few slow, deep, grounding, fortifying and reassuring conscious breaths. This action prepares, strengthens and orients you to the immediate task at hand, reduces stress and anxiety. Conscious breathing is calming to the central nervous system, oxygenates the prefrontal cortex and lessens the fight, flight or freeze autonomic responses. In the face of any challenge, draw a slow, deep breath to prepare. This slow, deep diaphragmatic grounding and centering breath will help instill confidence and recalibration.

Mindset: When you find yourself in a mindset, behavior or action that is not helpful, note the situation consciously, resolve not to be caught in that circumstance again. See yourself in a better way with the outcome you envision.

In Shape: Keep groomed, clean, neat appearance and your body in shape. Remain attentive to your appearance, health and hygiene. Use it, move it or lose it.

Deodorant: Instead of using deodorant, use instead the systems approach: reduce the acid formation in your body, reduce meat and cheese consumption putrefying in your digestive track, cleanse toxins, combine foods properly, reduce anxiety, minimize sugar, hydrate to cleanse and avoid constipation, eat a balanced diet and sleep soundly. No need for deodorant.

Nature: Being in and around nature will help to keep you grounded, honest and humble and reduce narcissistic tendencies in people with an exaggerated sense of self-importance since nature is bigger than they are especially when oceans, mountain ranges and sweeping vistas are involved.

Simple: Keeping things simple is the best approach. Maybe a little complex, but not too much so. As John Lennon said to his guitar players, "Not too many notes." "Simplify as much as possible but no simpler." —Albert Einstein

Sleep, Healthy Diet, Exercise: Nothing to explain here, just note. These areas are paramount.

The Smart Monkey Handbook:

Boredom: If you are experiencing boredom: that is on you, not the situation. Car drives, lectures, sitting around: find some meaning, purpose and ignite your imagination. Find something interesting to do, see, talk about, solve, think about, learn or enjoy. Meditate, remember, plan, be grateful. Even though we live in the United States of Entertainment, you don't have to make being entertained a major feature of your life. Being a constant consumer is an empty and lonely experience and an easy path to follow. Better idea: develop interests and become an amateur expert at something fun. This is very good for your self-esteem, and you will never be bored.

Time Alone: Spend time alone with your thoughts and feelings without entertainment or distraction, is a good way to know yourself. Self-reflection, free association of thoughts, using your imagination is a path to self-understanding. Solitude is instructive.

Your Opinion: Know your opinions and that your views and first impressions may change. Be willing to broaden your perspective, grow, adapt and change. "It ain't what you don't know that gets people into trouble, it's what you know for sure that just ain't so."
—Mark Twain

Breath and Anxiety: Cultivate the habit of drawing in a slow, calming, conscious breath from deep within your belly to the crown of your head. Diaphragmatic breathing will ground and center yourself with extra dose of oxygen. Every conscious breath will ensure your place in time and space and prepare you for what is coming next, reduces stress and replaces anxiety with feeling better. Let your breath make you free.

School: Elementary, middle and high school doesn't really last that long. It just seems like it does. It's not forever. Don't get too worked up over it. Learn what school has to teach, do well and prepare to move on. Learn about yourself, make friends and grow. Your life lessons will begin there, and real life begins to kick in halfway through college. Take advantage of all the school extracurricular programs you can: sports, drama, media, debate, cheer, travel soccer, mentoring, clubs, competitions, music, where you will learn more extracurricular lessons than in the classroom. Be patient, breathe, your real time comes later. Pace yourself for the longterm. Don't burn out in high school and misplace your priorities. While in school do the required work, as an exercise in discipline, not try to get out of things. You have a lot to learn.

Anger: If you blame others you give up your power and they control you. Angry people are fearful and feel alone. Have compassion for their unsettled souls and low self-esteem. Negative emotions reinforce each other and are unhealthy.

Problem: If you think you have a problem, think again, deeper. The problem you see is not the problem but a result of the problem. Again, use the broader, comprehensive systems approach to problem solving as well as life itself, not the cause and effect approach you learned as a child, which is too limited.

Depression: Depression is just another teacher for you and maybe one of your best. Depression is telling you to take care of your body, point of view and learn humility. You don't have a chemical imbalance which is a made up marketing term, stop eating so much sugar and improve your microbiome balance in the gut where neurotransmitters are made. Exercise, sleep and eating properly, think more broadly, be grateful, lend a hand to someone, have a goal and pursue it, reflect on your successes, admit and learn for your missteps and be more positive. Count your blessings. We all feel alone from time to time. Breathe some more. Do something. Help someone. Give something. Get something done. Finish it. Don't feel sorry for yourself for too long. Make a decision small or consequential. Follow through. You are still on the planet, and it is still spinning nicely. Act like you are glad to be here. Don't worry about your comfort and convenience for now, reach a larger goal. Your time will come later, be prepared.

Dig Deeper: There is always more to know. Half-truths, half stories, missing information, ulterior motives, profits being made, cover ups, hidden agendas, deception, whitewash, concealment, suppression, false front, outright lies, omissions, disguises and lack of transparency. Questioning, with a touch of skepticism is a good approach that will serve you well. Taking something at face value as presented can be disappointing, problematic and naive. It is always good to ask yourself what you are not being told.

What Goes Around: Pursuing a negative goal, hatred, wishing ill will or seeking revenge, vengeance, or harm may come back harshly on the perpetrator. Ensure that your motivations are pure with good intentions and focus on positive interactions in life. Paybacks, returned slights, recriminations, retributions, silence, getting even are all childish, specious and not a compelling path to self-understanding or enlightenment. What goes around, comes around.

Above Board: Always intend to do the right thing and you don't have worry or ruminate later over your decisions. Enough things can go wrong anyway when you follow the rules, laws and ethics. Sleep well without a guilty conscious by being decisive and making good ethical decisions in the first place. Do the right thing and you won't have to worry about it later.

Permanent Record: Your body keeps a permanent record of everything you see, touch, smell and experience. Just as with the legal system, social media, internet searches and government surveillance, nature records everything that happens to your mind and body just like the growth rings do on a tree in the forest. Old age holds the accumulation of the strains, shocks, abuses, trauma to the mind, body and spirit. Take care along the way to minimize the shocks and blows to the system, and help ensure a less severe old age with minimal wear and tear from noise, drugs, stresses, pollution, toxins, and smoke that take a cumulative toll.

Transitions

Start Young: It helps to start out very young with the thing you want to be good at: violin, gymnastics, second language, science, unicycle, tennis, or motorcross, so that you grow up developmentally with enhanced skills.

Lifelong Interests: Follow something all of your life to learn from it as it changes, and you will grow with it. Stay interested in things.

Not Difficult, Only Unfamiliar: Nothing is really difficult, just unfamiliar. When you stay with something and know it over time you make it your own.

Older You: You will need what you have developed in your youth when you are older and grow old. Keep that in mind when you are spending time and deciding what to accomplish. It is your hobbies that will comfort you and carry you through, not only the money you earn or the success you have. Everything is better enjoyed with personal development that you can share.

Give Time: Be generous, give time to other people and things. Two minutes or ten depending on the need but don't let anyone waste or steal your time. There are a lot of lonely people that will gladly take your time if you allow them. Determine what you need from an encounter and politely move on. In the end, time is everything and the only thing you need. How you use your time is a concept to master. The only time available is now so avoid squandering or wasting it while keeping in mind the John Lennon quote, "If you enjoyed the time you wasted, then it wasn't wasted time."

Travel: Travel as much as you possibly can and at any opportunity. Therein lies a good education. You will find your fears, insecurities, humility, prejudices, ignorance, information and areas to grow. You need to learn about the world by going places it in. The whole world is your home, not just the place where you are from. Take a world view not just regional or local perspective. You will thank yourself later when you are older and may not want to or be able to travel. No need to travel first class and be out of touch. Stay basic and travel more. Be international. The confidence, experience, independence and responsibility travel affords will make you more developed in every way. Travel has the capacity to open minds to the larger reality and improve both articulation of one's own point of view and to understand the point of view of others. The travel experience extends to all things. It's isomorphic. Nothing is going to happen to you sitting at home on the couch. So put down the cell phone and get off the couch. "Travel is fatal to prejudice, bigotry, narrow-mindedness and many of our people need it sorely on these accounts. Broad, wholesome, charitable views of men and things cannot be acquired by vegetating in one little corner of the Earth all one's lifetime." —Mark Twain. "The world is just a little town." —John Lennon.

Corners of Life: Nowhere is life more prevalent, precious, and acute than around the outlying edges where the most improbable story lines occur. The stories within the larger story is where the tectonic fault lines of meaning reside: in the cracks, crevices, quirks, and irregularities in the kitchen corners and odd coincidences of occurrences.

Non Stuckness: Move through a thing, area, mood, grievance, slight or emotion. Don't stay stuck but graciously extricate yourself with patience, grace, intention and by visualizing the outcome you want. Movement is what you need. "Nothing happens without movement." --Albert Einstein

Being Young: You are much smarter and more capable than you think or were taught to believe. You may just need a little more time, confidence from direct or vicarious experience and a larger fund of knowledge. Read more, do more, see more.

Cars: Recognize the serious responsibility that driving a car represents. You do not want to cause harm to a passenger, someone else or to yourself. 2000 pounds of a lethal surface projectile teeming with momentum requires a lot of time to stop and demands 100 percent of your constant attention outside the car to all rapidly changing conditions at all times. Look in both directions, twice. An instant is faster than you think. Cell phones, dogs, people, music, screens, mirrors are all potentially deadly distractions. It is easy to become complacent and lose sight of the danger involved while driving so remain focused; conditions change in milliseconds, reaction time is crucial. Having passengers in the car with you may be a fun time but they need to be paying attention to conditions outside the car also. Being responsible driving a car can extend responsibility to other areas of your life.

Isomorphic: Corresponding and similar in form and relationships, life also embodies many forms, metaphors, and similarities. "As in a grain of sand, is the universe."—William Blake

Rate of Time's Passage: Life starts out slowly, barely moves and a minute seems to take forever and then it drags on and gradually picks up and you become aware of time's passing and suddenly it picks up some more and you can't slow it down.

Years, then decades fly by and you wonder where it went and you are dumbfounded, unable to account for it all...so have something important for you to show for it as time excites and promises and paradoxically ravages and ultimately disappoints as it runs out as everyone but us knew that it would, someday. "Time waits for no one, and it won't wait for me." --The Rolling Stones. Time is the great tacit keeper of all things revered and feared, living and dead. Don't tempt it or play carelessly with it because sooner or later it will level you in one way or another and finally with finality. "If I could turn back time."—Cher

Costs of Being Young: While you are young, older peers may resent you and be jealous of your being young, naive and innocent. They may push you around, taunt, bully and play practical jokes on you. Be sure not to return that kind of immature behavior and when you get older and find younger people around, they will need a role model they can look up to. You may just be the role model for them.

Preliminarily Leave Home: Visit others, spend time away from home, stay with a friend or relatives overnight so you can get used to being away from home-safety and familiarity. Practice being on your own away from home while young. Then when you finally do leave home, you will be well practiced, and leaving will not be so difficult or traumatic. There are only three official phases of life keeping it simple: birth, death and leaving home.

Midlife Burnout: While there are three phases of life: birth, leaving home and death; there is a possible unofficial intermediate fourth life's phase, midlife burnout. Although midlife burnout is unlikely for you since you are reading a book such as this one which is intended to help prevent a midlife crisis. That phase would be: washing up half-drowned, disoriented and lost on the wind swept shores of mid-life crisis and burnout. This phase may be avoided by using the energy of youth, its innocence and ambition to develop purpose, meaning and balance for later in life.

Leaving Home: Of the three phases of life: birth, death and leaving home, leaving home may be the most challenging. There are many good coming of age movies from the 1970's and 80's. "American Graffiti" comes to mind. Also the controversial book "Catcher in the Rye." The old days are gone where you stay home on the farm and take it over or get drafted into a senseless war. All early life and development is in preparation for this stage whether we know it or not. Norman Lear said," Going is the easy part, it's leaving that is hard." You will need your parents much more after you leave home. Be sure you leave in a loving sentimental way and say goodbye properly, hug and not in the age-old traditional way, which is having a fight, either to hold back tears or to distract from the fact of a lack of preparedness or from years of pent-up anger. Make the leaving ok and reassure your parents they did a good job raising you, that they will be ok too and tell them you'll be fine while all the time knowing that after leaving home and for the next three or four years will be your most vulnerable years. Keep in touch, take good care of yourself and make good friends. Stay out of trouble. Tell them you'll be home for the holidays.

Wing and a Prayer: Get used to the idea that many of the best things are spontaneous, momentary and happen in an instant and then disappear far out of reach. So much depends on a whim, a flash, the thinest wisp of an idea and on the most unlikeliest of coincidences and a wing and a prayer. Notice the connection, grasp the opportunity and seize the moment. Carpe Diem.

Aging: No need to push growing up too fast. It happens on its own time. Puberty arrives way too fast and as soon as it does, aging begins, not just getting older.

On a Roll: Sometimes when you are pursuing an important task, are in a groove or are on a mission so to speak and very productively engaged, accomplishing something important that you want to see finished, it is helpful to stay buckled down and suspend most other non-essential activities until the job at hand is done in a reasonable time frame.

Phases: Life has many interests, areas, people, foods, fads, habits, obsessions, fashion trends, ideas, scandals and pastimes which are phases. Try to make the good ones last and the bad ones pass.

Routines: Routines are not boring. They are fixed known ways to get things done in an efficient automatic way. Spontaneity and experimentation in your daily living requirements are fine but a fixed, sure routine will get the job done. Waking up, getting ready for school, bedtime, homework, helping around the house, walking the dog, taking out the trash becomes grounding and reassuring and everyone benefits. Daily tasks get accomplished in a reliable way.

Problem Solving: Problems are not always the problem but the result of the problem. Use the systems approach not the limited linear cause and effect approach. For example: A problem is the child is misbehaving. Reframe the problem more broadly to: The parents are not disciplining effectively, consistently, establishing clear boundaries or providing positive expectations while tolerating poor behavior in the child. Another example: pimples are not the problem but a result of the problem which is: poor diet, hygiene or a stagnant lymphatic system. Symptom abatement is corrective systemically. Symptomatic treatment only relocates a problem as it becomes more acute and virulent later.

Elderly: Be kind and considerate of old people, they have been beat up, pushed around and have experienced much pain, loss and suffering that few will ever know. They have a lot to teach you, let them teach you compassion. You will be in their demographic soon enough. Avoid their pitfalls, absorb their wisdom. Listen to and learn from their stories. Guaranteed, no matter how many people are around them, they are profoundly lonely, profoundly lonely with little to look forward to.

Entering a Room: When entering a room with people, have presence, read it, make yourself at home and make eye contact. Depending on the setting be respectful or inconspicuous as required. Key your action, take your conscious breaths and begin to notice who and what is there and the prevailing mood. No need to be flamboyant or the center of attention. Engage with the space and make yourself comfortable. Begin to belong and enjoy yourself. Make the space your own. Act like you want to be there. Act like you belong there. Recognize, connect, be at ease and be present. Breath some more, talk to someone relatively soon, if possible, to connect and establish yourself without being intrusive, awkward or weird by imposing yourself uncomfortably on anyone just because they or are convenient or close by. If you are shy or introverted this open approach will help you grow out of feeling insecure and more toward extroversion. Wherever you are is where you belong, make a place for yourself. Your future spouse maybe watching you. Slightly timid but confident, with a healthy touch of humble self-conscious presence makes a good entrance. Much life occurs in the in between time and transitions.

Doors: This rock group made coming of age music for all times in the late 1960's. Listen to all of their albums. When you have accomplished that notice that you will feel differently and understand yourself even better. Then do the same for the Beatles. The groups are timeless and teach you more than you could ever learn on your own. Let them help you.

Success: It's going to take significant amount of time and an extended amount of effort. Playing the lottery is not a reliable plan for financial independence. No need to be a big Hollywood celebrity or a jet-setting mogul. A life that is meaningful with class and integrity that does some good would be better. Stand out, make your life mean something and don't just get by. Think highly of yourself and others will too. You will achieve what you expect. "Moderation is a fatal thing. Nothing succeeds like excess." —Oscar Wilde

Change: Change is the only thing that will not change and is a constant. If you find a solution and become too attached to it for too long, that solution will become your next problem.

College Degree: Those who have a college degree can be sure of one thing: they have a college degree.

Comfort Zone: If you are feeling out of your comfort zone, then expand your comfort zone. Don't be like a turtle and hide in your shell.

Breathe: Whenever you are feeling unsteady, anxious, conflicted, insecure or uncertain of your next move, always draw a deep diaphragmatic breath to center yourself and feel prepared for whatever is coming next.

Generations: As you may think your generation is it, this time is right, all things will be this way from now on, and all the out of touch old people don't have a clue, rest assured your time will pass too and the torch will pass to a new generation, and you will be sitting where the old are now.

Cockiness: Is useful, youthful and a kind of confidence.

Ask For Help: Don't be so timid and afraid that you don't ask for someone's help. You will need help and to give help all life through. Learn the rules and roles of helping and being helped, you will be able to accomplish so much more and so will the people you help. It is helpful to ask before helping someone.

Campaign: If you want something or want to get good at something it is helpful to mount a campaign of concerted effort over time. Hoping for what you want to drop in your lap is not a plan. Revise, define, refine, implement, plan and make what you want to happen by committing concerted and directed effort, over time, don't quit, no short cuts.

Getting Better: Hope is not a plan, but trust is a sacred pact that includes a plan. Trust that things will get better, that's where odds are in your favor.

Time/Money: However much time or money you think is necessary for a task, double it.

Establish Routines: With pretty much everything, there's a tendency to let a few things go until later or wait for another time to attend to some matter. We generally need to watch all things all of time and pretty much take care of everything. There is a lot to manage and monitor and more and more as you get older. Keep an eye on it all so nothing gets neglected or left behind. Keep an assignment book or to do list especially when deadlines are looming. You don't want to miss out, run out, time out or forget things or get left behind. Whether it's laundry, submitting an application, personal hygiene, practicing the cello, maintaining your health and diet, managing your growth and all of your responsibilities are important. You snooze you loose. Stay on your toes, blow your nose, wear clean clothes, careful if it glows, whatever you reap, you will sow, wind up the garden hose, meet at Moe's, watch how it goes, highs and lows, minimize the woes. "Nothing happens without movement." Albert Einstein

Physical Things and People: Any encounter with people and things are not always going to flow smoothly, cooperatively or predictably so be prepared and don't default to getting mad. Not much shows a lack of development more than someone getting mad at an inanimate object, not to mention people.

Next: Always be at least a little attentive to what is next, surprises are always best when prepared.

Waiting Too Long: Waiting too long is so common but yet a preventable hazard. There is a time, a slot, doorway, range of opportunity when action is optimal, perfect, just right, maybe a little sooner or a little later to strike. Too early or too late is definite and the opportunity is lost. Timing is often intuitive and not up to us. Check the schedule, call the friend, make the appointment, get the information, think ahead, make the call. Take the action, don't wait too long. Regret is best avoided in advance with well-timed action.

Good Advice

Tennis or Golf: Make a decision and pick one early on so you can be good at either or both. This will help in business and making friends and having fun in a well-accepted and social way. Later in life when you have more leisure time you will be glad that you have these skills to enjoy and to meet people having something in common. Be sure you learn to play the game of chess. It will structure, thinking and thinking ahead, problem solving, how to plan and how to change your plans. The lessons are universal, time tested and invaluable. Be a humble winner and a good loser. Isomorphic - similar in form, shape and structure...to all things.

Chess: Play and enjoy the game. It will teach you strategy, skills, develop your patience, mental mapping, thinking ahead and how to be a good winner and humble looser. Chess requires understanding your opponent's thinking, strengths and resolve. Thinking of five possible moves ahead improves your concentration, strategizing and decision making, all skills transferable to life. It is isomorphic.

Pop Culture: Following popular cultural too closely will become a distraction. You'll find out enough about it without even trying. Again, follow what interests you rather than just take what is marketed to you as a consumer. A better idea is to choose your own people and things to learn about. Choose your own role models past or present. Mark Twain, Carl Jung, Einstein, Muhammad Ali for example. They are time tested unlike pop culture celebrities.

Find Something: "Find something when you are young that can carry you through." John Densmore, drummer for the Doors

Personal Products: Avoid deodorants, skin care products, creams, perfumes as much as possible. These products are poorly regulated and contain toxic chemicals, much like in the fast and processed food industries. The regulatory agencies are regulated by the industries they regulate. Only a fraction of cosmetics and food additives have been tested for safety. This is not Germany. Many of the chemicals consumers are exposed to have been grandfathered in from decades earlier. If you have bad breath or body odor there is a systemic imbalance in your body correctable on the dietary or stress level that a deodorant, or worse yet, an antiperspirant won't solve: incorrect food combinations, stagnant lymph, accumulated toxins or poor digestion is a likely area for correction.

Musical Instruments: Always have a musical instrument that you can at least play a little to provide some comfort, grounding, enjoyment and continuity. When you are older and have become halfway proficient, as with tennis, golf or chess, it will be your friend and grow with you, remaining a companion throughout your life.

Corporate Media: Be aware and able to sense when the corporate media culture or controlling entities are hacking into your brain. Are you are being persuaded, brainwashed, being played for a fool to subscribe to a point of view or are being made compliant or buying things you don't need? Your point of view is purchasable by the media and your consent is manufactured. American capitalism is ruthless and predatory, although presented to you as nice, easy, glib, and fun for the whole family and packaged to you for your noncritical acceptance. Don't be asleep or sheep like and given to being fleeced. Misplaced trust is a common error and a con man's tool that makes us a willing victim. "It's easier to fool a man than convince him that he's been fooled."--Mark Twain. Americans like their familiar brand of B.S. flavored, sautéed, deep-fried and artificially sweetened with lies and a side of fries. It's apple pie and so hopefully delicious and seasoned to corporate perfection with a smile so reassuring as it kills, maims and injures. Don't be a victim lulled into complacency by blind trust. If you find yourself being seduced into a consumer-compliant stupor, recognize that you are being hacked, groomed, lied to and trained. There is always enough truth in a lie to seduce you into feeling good about what you are about to commit to or sign for. "Let me control and I will turn any nation into a herd of pigs."—Joseph Goebbles.

Basic Repairs: Learn to make basic repairs. The exercise is good for brain development. Blue collar is not beneath you. Everyone should be able to stop a running toilet. A sewing kit is useful to have.

The Law: Unless you are a lawyer avoid but have knowledge of the legal system in every day areas. It is unforgiving, final, expensive and unpredictable and its outcome outlasts a lifetime.

Read: Extensively and that does not include social media and buzz feeds. This will help you keep a larger perspective and broaden your language usage.

Advice: We all need all the advice we can give.

Practical Jokes: Most people do not like practical jokes.

Naiveté and Power Structure: Please disabuse yourself of any fairness belief in general and that the government cares about you and wants to help. The democratic system is an inconvenient nuisance for the power structure and often functions only as window dressing. If the system is caring, why so much demonstrating in the streets and litigation in the courts for our basic rights, freedoms, pensions and compensations? "I enjoy all the rights we used to have."—George Carlin. The billionaires, bankers and high-powered money interests take priority in any society and moves toward corruption. "Power tends to corrupt and absolutely power corrupts absolutely."—Lord Acton. "A leader must be concerned not only with reputation, but also must be positively willing to act immorally at the right times." -Machiavelli. As a country, we have been drifting away from our constitution and the Magna Carta, 1215 document establishing that the king and his government was not above the law, and giving up gradually our rights and freedoms that are now more window dressing, under the guise of exchanging freedom for security to protect us from the boogie man, who is really ourselves. First communism, then rogue states, failed states, then dictators backed and installed by our government, then terrorists, school shooters and now bad actors and microbes. Space aliens are coming to get you next in your lifetime. Our government ceased giving rights to taking rights away long ago. "Those who would give up essential liberty, to purchase a little temporary safety, deserve neither Liberty nor safety."—Ben Franklin. Land of the free, home of the brave but broken promises and treaties for the Indigenous Native Americans. It is beyond comprehension that nowadays and with such a painful history, we still have to fight for basic human rights and dignity that should be a given and could have been codified long ago: gay, women, civil, reproductive, health care, day care, informed consent, humane prison system, honest package labeling, corporate accountability, affordable housing, compassionate policing, accessibility to a responsive government for grievances and accountability for resolution on state, local and federal levels, objective news reporting, drug-add free television, no robo calls and timely, affordable court system judgements, etc.

Comfortable Baseline: As with many new things ahead, once a comfortable baseline is established, you can then carefully and confidently move on to more complex levels.

Preparing a Meal: Learn to prepare a few good healthy meals and keep improving until you are an amateur chef.

Thank You Note: Regardless of what decade you are living in, the practice of taking your time to send a thoughtful, handwritten thank you note will always be appreciated and speak highly of you. It is a timeless heartfelt action of appreciation and gratitude which reflects a sincerity that is hard to match by sending a fruit basket.

Be Nice: Be nice to other people, we have no idea of the pain and suffering they have experienced. They are on the planet for the first time too, with fear, insecurity and not knowing what to do.

18 things some people learn a little too late:

- Nature is not sentimental and will remove you in a split second
- Everything is temporary although it may seem otherwise
- Life does not need to be an exercise in difficulty and frustration.
- Life is not fair
- Prior planning prevents poor performance
- Family is most important
- People will treat you the way you treat yourself
- Under anger there is much fear, have compassion for angry people
- An angry person is temporally insane
- There will be no teaching or learning in anger
- Don't take anything personally
- Life only seems random
- Happiness is a choice requiring discipline
- A lifetime is not nearly as long as you think
- Always do more than is expected
- The biggest risk is not taking a chance
- Chance favors the prepared mind
- Things really don't matter so much especially in the end.
- You are free

Compliment: Help and compliment often. We all need a boost. Care about people, things outside of yourself. It is good for you to give a little. Don't be stingy. Reach out and ask if you can help.

One Time: If you take your time, know what you are doing, breathe, and perform a task carefully the first time you won't have to do it over again a second time. Saves time. "Take what you do seriously but not yourself. Do in haste, repeat in leisure."—Ben Franklin

Unknown Strangers: Many people may be reluctant to help an untested stranger or even a reference especially when their own reputation may be at stake. So, ingratiate yourself, be friendly, make new friends, make yourself known. Don't be a stranger, come forward, network, don't be shy, come out of the woodwork. Join groups, have fun, make contacts, make who you are, what you are about and where you are from, known. Show interests in others. Self-promote a little. No one really makes it on their own without some help. We all need a leg up and an outstretched hand down. Always leave a good impression. Smile, eye contact is important. Be complementary, positive and helpful. Introduce yourself. Have a good reputation, which always proceeds you. Help others and stay socially oriented and connected. Hold on to people and acquaintances, keep in touch.

Know What You Are Doing: If you are doing something and you don't feel that you really know what you are doing and there is safety, other people, danger or much money involved, stop before it's too late and something drastically goes wrong.

Something New: If you are trying something new, remember nothing is that difficult, just unfamiliar. Stick with it, it takes time to know something new and make it your own.

Keep up vs. Catch up: The former is so much more calm, satisfying and adult than the shabby out-of-breath-later. The adrenalin from coming up from behind is in the end, exhausting and over rated.

Just Once: Please note: often times some things, people and chances come by just once and only for an instant so stay vigilant.

Baldness: Baldness jokes or references are never funny or appropriate ever.

Sooner or Later: Usually the best time to do anything is sooner not later or better yet, now. Waiting for better timing is fine but not to be confused with procrastination.

Clean Up: A given task is not finished until the clean up is completed. Don't take all the glory and leave the clean up for someone else. This epitomizes weak character. No halfway jobs either. Take the task to completion and clean up too. If you are working in an organized manner, there will be little mess to clean up or tools to put away later. Clean up most of the kitchen before you sit down to eat. Clean as you go.

Home Stretch: Nearly the completion of a task is a good feeling. Be sure to follow through to the final step and not let up until the task is done. Many a task can go awry at the last minute due to inattention, complacency and taking the end for granted.

Good Things: Many good things are good, but only to a certain point.

Closing and Final Thoughts

Inner Light: The spiritual, mental, emotional, physical components of your life are all connected. Light, energy, wind, heat, touch, water, movement, space, breath and time connect everything and are your tools. Sleep, nutrition, body movement, health, meditation, wisdom, inner peace, enlightenment and relationships are your entitlements. Think big, take the high road, self-reflect and find purpose and meaning. Joy and happiness are a given, in plain sight and all around you. Gratitude will ground you, meditation will connect you. Give thanks. Breathe.

Take good care of yourself

Do good work

Keep in touch.

Dear Young Reader

Thank you for taking the time to read this book. What you've just read only scratches the surface of all the knowledge, concepts, and ideas there are for you to absorb. I encourage you to read the original book, The Smart Monkey Handbook: A Practical Guide for the Mind and Body, to continue to find more ways to grow, learn, and advance throughout your quest to become a happy and well-developed Smart Monkey. Don't forget to have fun during your growth.

Buena Suerta,

    Mark

Dear Older Reader

It has occurred to me that a few older readers, and parents may have picked up this book either to see what their kids are reading or if you feel you missed a point or two on your own growth journey or just to see where you they sit on the life lessons accumulations-spectrum. In any case I hope you've enjoyed reading the book as much as I enjoyed writing it. In the very least, I hope you found some reinforcement, solace and confirmation in the ideas provided, when compared to your own life experience. You may also find a laugh or two and a little sarcasm thrown in for good measure.

You may want to use this book by reading it along with your child; using it as an interactive exercise to promote healthy discussion and a check-in to observe and learn about your child's thoughts and feelings on any number of the topics in this book.

Mark Bodwalk

Mark

Notes

The following extra lined pages may be helpful to jot down additional points, thoughts, concepts, insights and ideas that will help you to continue to grow and have understanding.

Writing down ideas helps us to find meaning and remember what we are learning and want to make part of us. One of the pleasures in life is to take a new idea, understand it and make it your own.

When reading back over these ideas and experiences, you will feel a sense of encouragement. Always date your entries to see your growth journey.

About the Author

Born in Washington, DC to depression-era parents, the youngest of three brothers, who grew up in Northern Virginia, Mark attended high school in Miami Beach, Florida. After receiving a journalism degree from the University of Florida, and a high draft lottery number, 333, which allowed for a break (student deferment) from college, he began a serious interest in travel and living abroad that developed into a busy career in photography, working on a Mississippi River steamboat, and a long career as a Flight Attendant while simultaneously earning an advanced degree as a Psychotherapist, resulting in a decades-long clinical practice in Northern Virginia.

www.ingramcontent.com/pod-product-compliance
Lightning Source LLC
Chambersburg PA
CBHW060610080526
44585CB00013B/768